American Community Voices

Familial and Collegiate

Larry L. Didlo

DIAMOND MEDIA PRESS CO.
1-304-273-6157
https://www.diamondmediapressco.com/

ISBN Paperback: 978-1-951302-63-4

Contents

This paperback book is composed of four previously published e-books by AuthorHouse.com. It probably would be considered in the category or genre of non-fiction since it includes autobiographical text. The-e-books involved are about family development principles and ideas, plus reading literacy concepts. The photographs are from the family album mostly and news clippings from the past. As you'll probably agree after your first reading, some of the text is associated with a skewed curve in terms of frequency. How many people have the opportunity to teach overseas as a civilian for example?

The scouting awards and community service involvement, plus sometimes a global perspective, were derived from my teen years. Scouting is worldwide and enjoys the privilege of bringing young people together to share ideas and experiences in a positive setting. Scouting assisted me when delivering papers as a paperboy in JHS and helped me adjust to one of my first part time high school jobs. At 15, I was able to work in a retail store where my dad was the manager. Among other responsibilities, I trimmed windows viewed by pedestrians passing by the dollar store and worked behind the Store fountain or lunch counter. I recall my dad speaking about one of the manager's and assistant manager's specials: A bacon, lettuce, and tomato sandwich made with toast. That fountain special was rivaled when my mother boiled lobster tail and served it to her crew of five children with melted butter.

"B-P" of course is the George Washington of America in general terms when speaking of the scouting movement. Evangelist Billy Graham would probably also add that boy and girl scouts are beholden to all of its founders as well. I for one, nominated my father, or dad, to be on the James E. West Foundation Society list of the Twin-Lakes District within the Bay Lakes Council. My parents involvement at a Oshkosh local church fostered my receiving the God and Country Award a year after I was awarded the Eagle pin in Manitowoc at a Kiwanis Club Banquet. I accepted the religious award and recognition in Oshkosh after my dad was transferred from Manitowoc in 1955. My dad was among a very few individuals to encourage me to shoot for the highest award in scouting.

President JFK gave the 32nd Wisconsin National Guard a call-up for the

Berlin Crisis when I was enrolled in secondary education courses as a full time student and a Junior at the time... taking practicum or practice teaching in social problems classes at high school locally. This was during the Viet Nam era in 1961-62 at Fort Lewis Washington. More than ten thousand Wisconsin Guardsmen were later trained and considered a part of the US Army National Guard, after being activated in the fall of 1961 and returning. from Christmas vacation. The division didn't have to go overseas to Germany since it didn't escalate while the Berlin Wall was being put up. General Smith, the commanding General at the time, was in his later years. He did visit our company to deliver a speech. I was later assigned to the pool and gynmasium area as a PFC in special services. I was retrained as a Water Safety Instructor, or lifeguard for the pool by Red Cross personnel. I recall an interesting incident while guarding at the pool. A young lady in her swimming suit spoke to me about how she liked lady bugs. That reminds me of why America can be thankful to former President Teddy Roosevelt for his foresight in the early 1900's to preserve sites for our National Parks and tourist areas.

The previous paragraphs suggest why I want to dedicate this e-book consolidation into a brief paperback book. I want to be part of the 100 Anniversary of America Scouting as an educator and writer. I want to help preserve the scouting heritage of wholesome God and Country activities for the community-at-large, and to also promote global citizenship responsibilities through the proper use of the computer and technology.

When I returned from Europe as a civilian teacher-counselor and track coach at the Secondary level, I was lucky soon to find another faculty position at Elkhorn, Wisconsin. While in Germany, I was assigned to an Army Dependents School at the secondary level. This appointment or position was in conjunction with the Department of Defense or government. We didn't have the usual community elected school board to handle decisions at the administrative level in our host country on base. Fortunately I was then able to better understand my later position as a high school guidance counselor at Elkhorn High School. I was 28 years old when at Elkhorn and employed full time. You may want to compare that experience as written with my Jamboree experience sixteen years earlier. A good guidance question for students in their teens might be where and what would they like to be doing seven years from now? I was a fresh kid who was a second class scout and liked pancakes at the Jamboree. The words of then Vice-President Nixon who took the place of President Eisenhower seemed challenging when looking at three musketeers skit that followed his talk. All of the 50,000 Scouts that were gathered near Los Angeles on the many peaks and sides of the sand dunes also lit a candle in the darkness that evening, making quite a spectable to experience. The Manitowoc Aluminum Goods Manufacturing Company donated aluminum neckerchief slides for all the scouts attending from that area. Patches and neckerchief slides were traded or swapped in the large tents pitched in the valleys of the sand dunes. Such interaction or experience meeting teens from other states and countries helped me develop a more positive attitude toward my own age group and general public later in my career as an educator and security guard. Camp experiences with church folks, fellow scouts and YMCA members provided valuable insight.

Recently, although presently semi-retired from professional education employment, I returned to graduate school in Oshkosh for four years as a part-time graduate student in the School or College of Education at UW-Oshkosh, Curriculum Studies K-12 with an emphasis on diversity courses in the K-12 Curriculum. I wanted to upgrade my teaching credential and work toward a second masters even though I was retirement timber. I want to emphasize the importance of experience and education in learning. It's not just for students of John Dewey popular after WWII. This is also illustrated in TV's Samantha Brown's travelogues. She travels around the world with her camera crew and samples native cuisine, speaking with the locals about interesting places to visit for sight seeing. On foot, bicycle, or trolley, and perhaps even a four-wheel drive Mule gives the TV audience insight for future trips and so forth. Prague was one of the places where snitzel was prized (hot dogs) and architecture from different centuries and countries (e.g. Baroque) were preserved untouched from WWII.

Part of the purpose of intorducing this new paperback is to emphasize the Scout's Motto: Be Prepared. In other words, be prepared to save time for as much education as possible, or think in terms of survival in a strange place such as hunting if you become lost. After going through some of the hoops or think in terms of survival in a strange place such as hunting if you become lost. After going through some of the hoops or ropes of scouting (badges and volunteering as an adult merit badge counselor) one must not forget about the U.S Constitution.. it is written! Also, for those that accept the challenge, they may want to run for public office, or atleast register to vote!

My bid for the local Oshkosh School Board, City Counsel and State Assembly went down in defeat, unlike my Badger Boys State experience when I was a high school Junior running for Lt. Governor at Ripon College. I was sponsored by the local Rotary Club and it helped prepare me for the role of Student Council President my Senior Year at Oshkosh High School in 1958. However, I must admit that teaching Language Arts at the 7th and 8th Grade levels and high school government Classes are not the same as getting elected for public office, but as the motto suggests, it helps one to be prepared just like a college education, married or unmarried.

What are some of the community organizations that promote democracy, or go beyond the village concept of Hillary's book. Perhaps some would point to Goodwill Industries Thrift Stores, the DAV, VA, Eisenhower's People to People Citizen Ambassador Programs, The American Legion, VFW, BSA, Community Y, Rotary, Elks, Kiwanis, Badger Boys State and other altruistic community based organizations, along with church groups and more humanitarian based groups as the Red Cross. While being interviewed for one of the district State Assembly Seats in Madison, I was challenged on local TV to give my opinion on questions and issues written about in local and national newspaper and sometimes ignored sometimes because of lack of interest or understanding before voting on referendums and candidates.

Before closing, this educator-writer would like to give credit to an unselfish act of a fellow now Eagle Jamboree Scout while riding to California on a Greyhound Bus many years ago. His name is Bob, and Bob received his Eagle when 14 also. Actually, when you think of it Sam Walton of Walmart also delivered newspapers as a young boy and also when attending the university, and got his Eagle when only 13 years old. Bob loaned me his Kodak Box Camera and helped me launch a lifetime hobby of photography, especially on sightseeing trips away from home. I still have photos of Yellowstone National Park and

Mouont Rushmore taken while going to the California Irvine Ranch National BSA Jamboree in 1953.

Some of the post-secondary schools attended the last 50 years include the following: UW-Oshkosh and Indiana University-Bloomington. I received a M.S. in Education form IU-B, and a BS in Secondary Education majoring in Social Science... at what is now renamed University of Wisconsin-Oshkosh.

Wise Men Seek Him

Larry L. Didlo

by John Didlo, Sn & Larry Didlo © pending '07, Jan

Prologue

Intorduction to life story: overview & comments by eldest son.

After letting the dust settle on this manuscript about my dad's life, I've decided to publish it on the Internet with 1st Books because I think it is relevant in today's more technological oriented world. My mother three electronic books speak of family life in general, but this account written twenty-one years ago, six years before "Mr. D" passed away is very special to me in an age where it may not be such a good idea to forget the past and the lessons we may learn from it. My dad wrote this edited autobiography beginning in 1980 at 77 years of age. He began at his desk at home in Oshkosh, Wisconsin. I've been associated with the local university as a night student for several years taking credential renewal courses in reading education. I value this manuscript not only because my dad was a good role model along with my mother, his wife, but also valued higher education and helped put me through college, as he did with his own brothers, Chet and Ray in Minneapolis. My dad, or father, completed this manuscript in 1981 and passed away six years later. Before ending this introduction, I would like to again just emphasis the significance of being able to get published on the Internet. Just like a nametag in church or at a church camp, getting published inexpensively opens doors for many who wouldn't otherwise be able to benefit from the more common avenues of awareness and understanding. As President of St. Lawrence Consortium Education Foundation, I think this autobiography is helpful to better understand former generations and their environment. SLC is a non-profit organization that began a few years ago publishing a 39 volume series of newsletters mostly to relatives and educational associates, about reading literacy, plus current and past events here in the USA and abroad. Family shots are available on the Internet website: www.picture.com Type in didlo and clock search!

In closing, as somewhat the overseer of my dad's work, I have my dad to thank for sparking my interest in JHS in golf, sailing, the BSA Eagle Scout Program, and enabling me to appreciate the power of leisure time reading.

Cordially,

Larry L. Didlo, M.S. Ed IU-B ' 64, Phi Delta Kappa

Educ. Fraternity, Who's who in the Midwest-

Marquis 1998-01 (Millenium Edition) I.B.C.

(Intern Bio. Centre, Cambrigge, England, 2001) and

A.B.t. (American Biographical Institute) 1000

Leaders of the World Influence 2001.

Autobiography of John Harvey Didlo

I was born on May 13, 1904, one of nine children born to William Didlo and Margaretter Sollars Didlo. I was born on a small farm west of St. Jospeh, Missouri in a community known as French Bottoms. Many French families settled in this community of 4,000 acres. It was bounded by the Missouri River and known as French Bottoms.

My grandfather, Nicholas Didelot, immigrated from Alsace Lorraine, France, via Switzerland and Canada. He drifted down through the United States landing in good spirits in St. Jospeh, Missouri. There he met Pauline Colome who had also immigrated from France with her sister, Mary Colome. Both worked their way over on a ship by waiting on table and doing housekeeping. When Nicholas and pauline first met, the two sisters were working in a boarding house. Nicholas and Pauline eventually married. Mary wed Joseph Dupree and both families signed up for a farm under the Homestead Act in the 1870's. these farms are now owned and operated by their grandchildren.

My folks operated a family farm. Our family then owned three or foour cows for milking and meat. We also raised a litter of pigs each year, which were then butchered and smoked as needed. After building our own smoke house, we could smoke bacon and hams, etc. THe family usually had two teams of horses to use. Chores were delegated to the children by the time they reached the age of seven or eight.

My older brother, Arthur, took care of the horses, plowing, planting and harvesting along with the younger children's help. I took care of the cows and chickens. I did the milking with the help of one of my younger brothers. I also refurbished a chicken house for setting hens. Each year we raised about one hundred chickens and had chicken every Sunday.

The next brother in line after me was Oliver who, with the help of Chester, fed the hogs. This consisted of cutting weeds and tossing them over the fence and seeing that the hogs got enough water of slop, and corn.

We raised potatoes, turnips and at least twelve varieties of apples kept in cool caves for the winter months. The cabbage we raised was shredded and put in a barrel-together with salt at the top. Dad put a weighted lid on top which compressed the cabbage and made wonderful sauerkraut.

We also planted corn, some of which after harvesting was ground into corn meal and then cooked into corn meal mush. The cereal was heated and eaten with milk and sugar. This could also be set aside to settle, sliced and fried, and served with bacon and eggs. I believe our meals were healthier thatn today's prepared foods.

My dad and all his sons hunted and fished as a sport, eating most of the game bagged. We were taught never to shoot or kill anything unless we need-ed it for food, i.e., unless it was something like a chicken hawk or coyote! No hunting or fishing license was needed in those days.

Never will I forget some of Dad's remedies for our family. For example, whenever one of us had an earache, the home remedy was to go out and ger a cottontail rabbit, dress it out and empty its bladder into one's ear while the urine was still warm. The remedy for tonsillitis was a one or two pound bag of fresh warm or hot cow manure. It was placed under the chin and tied above our heads. And worn all night. Dad must have learned about these remedies from his Mom who probably brought them over from the old country I will probably never know, nor will I ever forget them.

Neither will I forget the old, white headed medicine man, Mr. Murray, who made the rounds in his horse drawn buggy visiting the French Bottoms farms every two or three months. This was quite an event and we nine kids would gather around and watch when he opened his grip and displayed his wares. Dad bought turpentine for the farm animals and used it for fresh cuts to keep flies off and prevent infection. He also bought the cough syrup with the pictures of the famous bearded Smith Brothers (no Dopey the beardless dwarf pictured) on the box.

My mother passed away in 1917 when I was thirteen years of age. My old-est brother, Arthur, was then seventeen and my old sister, Lorena, was fifteen. She had to drop out of school and take over the household duties, with the help of Lilian, who was then eight. My Mother died of a miscarriage at the age of thirty-seven. She had had three previous miscarriages. She had a total of nine children from ages one and one-half years old to seventeen. Taking care of all us kids, cooking for the family and doing the household duties might cause any woman to have a miscarriage. I remember churning the butter, helping with the washing, and chopping the kitchen stove wood that kept the woodbox filled. We had a pot bellied stove in the center of our living room which was used to heat our home. It was sort of a way of life then, again today becoming popular with the present price of heating oil and gas. My two sons, John and Bill, who live in northern Wisconsin, have wood burning stoves also.

I would like to make this comment which I heard from our present family doctor who recently retired. "The trouble with women today is that they don't have enough to do compared with sixty years ago, in the early twenties. Everything is 'push button', cooking, washing and sweeping." He also said that the food is canned or frozen and meat is cut into steaks, hamburgers and even TV dinners. To make things worse, they want their hubby to do the dishes and change the babies "diddies."

I attended a country grade school. After twelve years of age, my school year started in January due to the fall harvest. We had fifty apple trees that needed picking and storing. Corn, like peas, had to be cut and shuck. Potatoes were dug and stored, fields plowed, hay cut and stored in the barn. Besides, neighbors needed some hired help and it gave us a chance to earn some money. My first job paid me 50¢ per day for ten hours work plus my noon meal. This was during the hay harvest. When I was eleven years of age, and in my second year of working outside of home, my Dad said "Harvey, you have to ask for a raise." This was hard or difficult for an eleven-year-old kid to do, but I swallowed my pride, walked up to the boss and said, "From now on, Mr. Chance, I will have more money." "How much?" he asked. "Seventy cents per day" I replied. The boss didn't say anything until the day's work was done and then he said, "Won't be needing you anymore young man." This was the first and last time I was ever fired.

Our grade school teachers were very strict, but they did not have any of the trouble that one hears about today. I studied long and patient hours in that old grade school. One teacher back then might teach from forty to sixty children from the first to the eight grade. When I was in the eight grade, at sixteen years of age, our old German teacher inspired the eight grade class to graduate and become teachers of little men and little women. We all buckled down and believe it or not, we all graduated. I decided to continue on to hight school. It was a two mile walk every morning and every night. However, I stuck to my guns, played football, basketball, baseball, and also went out for track and field events. I believe I was born with a strong constitution. I thought the fresh country air and exercise would help me reach the age of ninety at least. Never understood why people smoked-breathing that filthy smoke into their lungs, so I decided that I would never smoke. Had two wonderful uncles on my Mother's side who took to drink and I saw how utterly pitiful and helpless they looked when intoxicated and I decided that was not for me. I also read articles on smoking and drinking and discovered what it did to a person's liver and lungs. This helped me to follow the straight and narrow path of healthy living. Sure, I'll have a beer, glass of wine, or a highball, but not too often. We have had the same six-pack in our refrigerator for months now.

When I was seven years of age in 1911, I was playing in our yard and there was a big ball of fire that came from the west, traveling in an easterly direction. A few seconds later there was a loud popping and banging noise that followed what I would now call a meteor. This meteor lit up the earth all around me and scared the hell out of me and Mum. Don't remember or recollect anything else about it.

Another event in my boyhood days that seems to stay in my mind was a Missouri River swim. Marvin Weiss, my cousin at seventeen, was learning to swim. I was fifteen then and Oliver, my brother was thirteen, and Chester age ten, went down to teh old muddy Missouri River for a swim. I swam out the farthest, Oliver was next and Chet third. Marvin was to swimm along the bank. We three swam approximately 100 yards out in the channel and Marvin began to yell for help as the current had hit the bank where we were swimming. He was swept out into the main channel. By the time I swam to shore and ran back and dove in toward Marvin, he was clutching a six foot long two inch limb, going down for the third time. I know I swam over him, then down under the water and at one second touched his body. Unfortunately, I was too exhausted to stay under the water that long, and had to surface and swim ashore almost drowning myself. His body was found floating down river five miles away a week later. Marvin's sister, Estella Weiss and I had dinner at their old farm in St. Joseph in February, 1981 (the year this autobiography was written) and discussed the tragedy. Estella is now 76 years of age and is the only one living on their part of the former Didlo estate. She never got married. Estella still fishes in the Missouri River, has a garden and cans all the vegetables and fruit she needs. One of her cousins, Harvey Dupree, farms her crops on shares as he does ours also.

During high school vacations, I worked one summer in the Mueller Keller Candy factory I worked another for the Ives Ice Cream Company, helping make ice cream and delivering it. The last summer high school vacation I took a job with classmate in his brother's rock quarry making little ones out of big ones. At times, I made as much as $4.00 per day. this quarry was located on a hillside northwest of St. Joe, overlooking Chicago, Burlington and Quincy Railroad. Day after day, Al my buddy and I, watched the Chicago, Burlingtoin and Quincy go by as we worked. This railroad was quite lenient with hobos or tramps who rode on their freight trains. These itinerant workers were heading for the harvest fields. I always wondered what was beyond those hill of the Midwest. Al and I finally hopped a freight and headed west before deciding on a regular vocation.

We were able to buy a new pair of overalls, a cowboy hat and shirt, and stuffed some money in the waistband of our trousers before catching a freight. Our destination was western Nebraska where the wheat harvest was about to start during the mid-twenties. We had our problem with "homos." We didn't know then to knock oit off or we would knock the hell out of them. Al and I kept to ourselves and eventually landed in Sidney, Nebraska. We bought a dozen rolls, a hunk of bologna sausage, a loaf of bread and struck out a foot over the country roads sometime in July' 1925. We came to a big wheat farm, where they were assembling a wheat combine. After introducing ourselves to a Mr. Ralph Harlan, we told him that we were Midwestern farmers looking for work. Ralph took a liking to us and said he would have his old lady put another potatoin the pot!

Yeah, I still remember that day. Al and I had spent the night before sleeping in an empty boxcar. It was sure cold that night sleeping on the boxcar floor. We were much closer to the Rocky Mountains haf realized. During that afternoon, assured of a job, I went over to the pump and got a drink. We sat down in the sun and slept until Rudy Harlan called is to supper. The next day we went to work. Al drove the tractor and I handled the combine. We finished his farm and Ralph got others to harvest. Al and I spent the rest of the summer working for him at $4.00 per day which was sent home.

When the harvest was over, Ralph, Ruby, and Doris (age two) decided to drive to Denver, Colorado. They invited Al and me to go along. We accepted. We spent a couple of days there and when the Harlan's headed back to Sidney, Nebraska, Al and I hooked or hopped, a freight train headed for home.

I corresponded with these people ever since that year. Ruby passed away in 1970. Doris, the daughter, was about 47 years of age then and decided to move back home with her dad and keep house for him. She never married. I visited these folks during 1975 on my way out to the Southwest near the Phoenix area. We talked of old times and looked over some snapshots taken fifty years ago. Ralph took me down town and introduced his friends. He had given up the farming years. Both he and Ruby had bought a home in Syney. Ralph was 85 years of age at this time and I was 71 (6 years before writing this article). Doris was 52 years old and her hair had turned silver. Ralph passed away in 1977. Doris became a minister in a small church in Enid, Oklahoma. We still keep in touch. I'll bet that some day she will have a church in Sydney, I sure hope so.

When I got back in St. Joe, I reflected on my childhood days when we kids saw our first car, We had two water spaniel dogs for which brother Arthur made harnesses. He also built a play wagon using baby buggy wheels. Our home was about one quarter of a mile from the dirt highway. The doctor sometimes had to come out to the Bottoms with his new Maxwell automobile. I happened to be in the wagon (at about age six) holding the reins. When Art saw the car he hollered, "Sic em!" Boy, did I have a fast ride in that wagon. It's a good thing the dogs stayed on the road.

Sure I fell in love with a farm girl in my late teens and we became engaged, however my chosen vocation took me away from home. Although we stayed in touch for several years, I drifted. Absence makes the heart grow fonder-perhaps even for someone you might meet later in life.

When I got back to St. Joseph in 1925, I decided to go on to college. Early in Spetember, about 1925, I went to the local Junior College to enroll. I was told that I needed credits in Latin and Algebra, neither of which I had taken in high school. I told the registrar that I didn't need Latin since I was going into the business career field and although I wasn't the brightest student in English, I could understand it. It was a stop sign for me! I didn't want to waste my time on Latin and Algebra. Consequently, I went to the library, found some books on how to write a good application for an employment letter and got busy on my old typewriter. I had taken a commercial course in high school which included book keeping, commercial law, commercial geography, shortland, English and tyoing. I prepared myself for a business career and low and behold, the two best answers I received wete from F.W. Woolworth and S.S. Kresge Co. One of the companies offered me $15.00 per week and that was F.W. Woolworth Co. of Levenworth, Kansas. The S.S. Kresge Co. offered me $22.50 per week and it just happened that the S.S. Kresge Co. superintendent was in the Kansa City store when I was interviewed. He introduced himself and interviewd me. After chatting a spell, he asked me where I wanted to work. When I told him to give me a week and I'd be there with my "spurs" on-it was a deal.

I really hit the ball the first week and the manager came to me with my first pay envelope, telling me that I had done good work. They would be paying me $25.00 per week. You know, I couldn't believe that I was going to make over $4.00 per day, six days per week. I couldn't see how they could afford it.

In the next two years I learned to trim inviting windows and make colorful displays. Eventually I became a part-time floorwalker besides my regular stockroom responsibility. After being in the business one year I was transferred to the floor as a floor-walker and merchandiser. One of my jobs was to catch shoplifters and believe me, I caught plenty of them. Another job was to teach new girls how to handle their department. After walking in the store for several months, I got my buddy, Al Seitz into the stockroom. We used to go to St. Joe on Saturday nights, and on Sundays, fishing in the Missouri River or hunting in the woods. One day we had plans for a get-together in St. Joe during September, 1926. Al was to leave Kansas City in Sunday with the 4:30 a.m. inter-urban but I wanted to leave earlier that Saturday night, which I did. Many times afterwards I wish I had gone with Al, for we never saw "Al" alive again after that.

Six months later I saw an article in the Kansas City Star. The headline asked about whose body lies in such and such a grave? The body that was supposed to have been buried there had resurfaced in another part of the country alive! Six months earlier Alfred Mast had written his wife a note saying "I am going to commit suicide and you will find my body floating down the Missouri River." When the body was found it was buried as Alfred Mast. And then, six months later, the real Alfred Mast showed up in Indiana. I had written to the Harlans, in Sidney, Nebraska, to friends living in iowa, called all Kansas City hospitals and had done everytthing I could to locate my associate and friend, Al. When I rad that shocking headline, I decided to take the vest of the suit Al had worn (before he disappeared) and go to the police in Kansas City. They hadn't done anything to locate Al. When I went to the chief that day he said that I should go to the newspaper and show them what I had, and tell them my story.

I went to the newspaper and they started right on the case. They called his parents first, had the grave dug up the next day and called the dentist at the University of Missouri for questions about pictures of Al's dental works. To make a long story short, it was my friend Al's body. He was buried in St. Joseph in his family cemetery plot. No evidence was ever found against the Alfred Mast who said he was going to commit suicide. He had commited a forgery and he disappeared to beat the rap. We assumed he may have murdered Al Seitz for the $80.00 Al had with him. Later I was taken to look at Alfred Mast while he was in jail for the forgery, but I had never seen him before and no one had any evidence against him. One of these days I am going back to the Kansas City police and show them the scrap book I have on this murder to see of anything was ever found abour Al Seitz's strange disappearance and death. I suppose the only way that anything could be found out is through a guilty conscience and a confession by the culprit who committed the crime.

When Al Seitz disappeared after a week of work, a Kresge manager asked of I had another friend that wanted to be employed. I did have another friend with whom I had gone to grade and high school. I brought Leonard Sanders down to the store and he was hired. He went to work for the Krege's store in Kansas City in 1927 about two years after I was hirted. Leonard enjoyed the work and eventually became a Krege manager of several stores: one in Duluth, Minnesota, and another later in Sheboygan, Wisconsin. He wound up as a manager in Watertown, Wisconsin, where he died of cancer in 1963. I was best man at Leonard and Madeline's wedding in 1928 on St. Joseph, Missouri. When Leonard passed away in 1963, Madeline sold their Watertown home and moved to Minneapolis where their daughter lived. Madeline died of cancer in 1976 in Minneapolis, Minnesota. her daughter was employed buy the Kmart Company and the last time I heard she was Personnel Manager.

After working at the Kresge store on Main Street in Kansas City for 2 1/2 years, I was transferred to the Fort Madison, Iowa store. As assistant manager, i earned $27.50 per week during the first six months of 1928. I made some very nice friends in Fort Madison. We met at a home where mid-day meals were served at 50¢ per meal. School teachers and business men met there with the five of us usually gathering around a table for lunch! These men were Hi Grey, Advertising Manager of Schaefer Pen Company; Les Beals, Assistant Advertising Manager of Schaefer Pen; Jerry Humphrey, of the highway department; Sam Bodwin of the Light, heat and Power Company and myself. We fellows have kept in touch with each other and visited each other. Les Beals and I are the only survivors at this time. Les and Betty Beals retired in 1967, selling their home in Syracuse, New York and then investing in a Boca Inlet apartment at Boca Raton, Florida.

Les Beals later advanced to Advertising Manager of the Lyon Healy Company of his hometown Chicago, Illinois. When he bid me farewell to me in Fort Madison he told me that if I ever was transferred to Chicago, I should let him know and perhaps I could stay with his family.

Two months later I received a wire to report to the S.S. Kresge store at 1029 East 63rd Street in Chicago. I called Les and he met me at the depot and took me home with him. The store was only four blocks form his house. What a Godsend-having someone meet this country boy at the depot and then inviting him to his home. I stayed with Les and his parents for nine months. The

Beals were marvelous people!

I was later transferred to Kenosha as an assistant at the same salary, but at a lot better store. I stayed there for six months and in January, 1930 (26 years old) I was transferred back to Chicago as manager of Store #408 at 79th and Halsted Street.

I managed this store for two years and then was transfered to Minneapolis, Minnesota in April, 1932 as manager od store #134 at 415 Nicollet Avenue. One was paid according to how much net profit the store made. My salary while in Minneapolis was between $3,000 and $3,500 for the five years between 1932 and 1937. I lived at the Minneapolis Y.M.C.A for five years. There was a young lady representative of the Armond Drug Company out of Des Moines. Iowa that visited my store. We fell for each other. After going out to dinner we went out dancing while she was in the area making calls on other stores. That was it... we became engaged!

Then in July, 1937, I received a call from Mr. Kresge to report to store #420 in Manitowoc, Wisconsin. This was a sad farewell. i had been manager in Minnepolis for five years, had many friends and built up a wonderful organization. I played on half a dozen excellent golf courses and had good hunting grounds available around or near the twin cities. Pheasant and deer were plentiful. I hated to leave the Minneapolis-St. Paul area as I had helped two brothers living and attending college there. Chester eventually graduated from Minnesota University, and Ray from Macalester College. "MAC" at St. Paul, was a Presbyterian college founded before the Civil War, focusing on the arts, sciences and music. Ray was involved with sports as an upper classman.

Store #420 in Manitowoc was a profitable store and it paid off. My salary started at $4,000 and eventually grew to $14,000. Clara M. Wood was a representative of Armond Cosmetic Drug Company and was from Des Moines. We were married on Thanksgiving Day in 1937 at the First Presbytarian Church in Des Moines, Iowa. Ten months later the young lady, Dee Anna, who first typed this autobiography was born to us.

In the next 10 years we had four more children and I would say they all had a happy childhood. We always had a real Christmas. good holidays, birthday parties and vacations. I don't believe any of my children ever touched dope. I have never asked them, I simply told them how dangerous and terrible it was to get the habit. I took the boys fishing and hunting in Manitowoc and Oshkosh. The girls got married before they got out of college and John Jr. was married aas soon as he got out of high school. He joined the Navy for a few years and owns his home in Clam Falls, Wisconsin. He works for the telephone company in the neighboring area. In fact, all of our children own their homes.

Bill, my youngest son, got married last October (1980) and also lives near Clam Falls. He had experience as a real estate broker and loves the northwoods where he and I still go deer hunting every fall when I am in Wisconsin. We both got our bucks last year on the second day of the season while hunting on his hardwood acreage.

I retired in 1969 and one year of retirement was all I could take raising a garden and watching t.v. Perhaps Phoenix, Arizona was to be my next challenge!

My brother, Ray Didlo (who was a broker in Phoenix) kept writing and calling me to come out to the Southwest to join him. This I did in the fall of 1971 and went to real estate school. I took the state exam and passed it early in 1972. I joined his firm and found a lot easier way to make money than running a dime or dollar store in Manitowoc, or K-mart later in my business career.

In order to make money in real estate one should know about what he is investing in enabling him to resell for a profit. One sells real estate for a comission, but there are occasions when one may see a good buy to hold for resale. I know I make more money buying and selling after holding for resale, than selling on commission. I bought land and resold the same, and did likewise with two houses. I would not advise any young person to go into real estate and do as I did. Remember, I was in business for about fifty years previously and had goine through the depression. I was with a reliable company where I built up a pension, plus social security. Even if I had lot my shirt in real estate, I could still get by. Real estate can be tough on a person without outside income especially in times like these. Still, there are people out there with money to invest.

Back in 1929 I recall that I had saved every nickel I could and invested it in the stock market. Things weren't "flying" very well in the late twenties, a few years Linderberg flew to Paris. In the depression I lost my shirt as did many others in our company, or for that matter, any other company at that time.

I remember I was managing in Chicago at the time and fully invested in the stock market. My friend and former manager, Russ Bailey, bought a Chicago apartment house. Another Kresge manager said he was going to play it safe and put his money in the bank, which he did. Here is what happened-my stock went down to zero and everyone moved out of Bailey's apartment house. Consequently, Bailey couldn't make the payment or pay his taxes, so he lost by foreclosure. THe manager who put his money in the bank also lost out. The bank went bankrupt and paid him twenty cents on the dollar. I sold my stock and lost my shirt!

I was fourteen years of age when Worls War I broke out. This was the age that I first made a man's wages driving mules in hay harvest. I remember our first big pay day, my elder brother Arthur and I, earned more than $100 and took this home and proudly presented it to our Dad, who made good use of it with a family of nine kids.

When World War II broke out I was managing the Manitowoc store and was about 35 years old. Clara and I had 2 or 3 children at that time of our life. Htat draft board listed me as #H#, whatever that meant. I did not have to go to war. I ran the East-Central Wisconsin store with my organization of girls and one sixteen year old boy.

As far an elections are concerned, I have always wished that Senator Goldwater, after JFK was in office, would have been elected and gone into the Vietnam War to win and bombed hell out of Hanoi. Those :gooks" or "cukes" are still probably killing and shooting each other. There were also starving women and children involved in civil strife. Sometimes war, although not the best solution, is more expedient.

My health is better than the average person at my present age of 77. I hope to live to be from ninety to a hundred and still feel good. Although I can't jog as far as I used to, I sleep longer and tire faster. I still like to wrestle but don't care to box anymore. I eat food that is good for me. Like other city folks we like oatmeal, and sometimes toast, for breakfast at least four times a week. It's been over sixty years now and love it.

I still haven't learned to smoke and don't believe I ever will. However, I do have a glass of wine or bottle of beer at least once a month. We have hemp weed down on the Didlo estate which is what is used to make marijuana. On the other hand, boaters and sail makers sometimes use hemp fibers to make excellent sailcloth! However, the dried leaves and flowers of hemp can also be rolled up in cigarettes and smoke. I was down in St. Joseph last month and burned off a patch of the hemp weed along the riverbank. What is your pleasure?

My advice to young people of today is to choose a vocation that they will enjoy and make life challenging. If one works for a big corporation, choose one with lots of fringe benefits and a good pension for retirement.

Another thing to remember is to take good care of that body of yours, it's the only one you are ever going to have. Remember Apostle Paul and Corinthians? Smoking will shorten your life, perhaps cause cancer. As you know, too much alcohol will ruin the liver and also shorten one's life.

THE GROWING YEARS, by J.H. Didlo, Sn. (Harvey) and Edited by Larry L. Didlo. Larry was defeated in the Primary Election of Republican Candidates September 12th, 2006 in Oshkosh, WI. He ran for State Assembly Seat of the 54th District. This educator turned politician for a spell draws on the memory of his family album of photos to the theme of WISE MEN SEEK HIM.

Revised copy © pending 2007 Appendix to Harvey's Autobio

*Appendix to J.H. Didlo autobiography written to theme of
Wise Men Seek Him Reflections.*

*Dedicated to the Ammerican Scout Program of the past,
present, and future! C/o Editor Larry Didlo*

Grandpa William Didlo is taking a break from the French Bottom Farm chores in this photo from the family album. He is passing the time with a few friends that dropped by to visit near St. Joseph, MO.

Dad (Harvey) Didlo kneels with a loyal companion of his younger growing years.

*Role playing a guiding force at about one years of age at the
Dildo Farm. The editor now seeks more wisdom in cultivating
ideas instead of soil for the better future of mankind, with
a touch of leadership or just a spelling book at hand.*

*This photo of the Didlo Clan in the Twenties seems to capture several smiles.
All but Chet and Rey are gathered. They are in the "football"
line however seen later.*

Food on the wagonside after a great hunt.

This photo was taken about the late forties on the Bottoms Farm.

This snapshot of the Twenties depict some of the equipment and young men harvesting wheat in Nebraska. Harvey and a companion rode the freights (empty boxcars) to find part-time work during summer months. He was able to save some money and acquire more farm skills away from home, before landing an interview with the SS Kresge personnel recruiter.

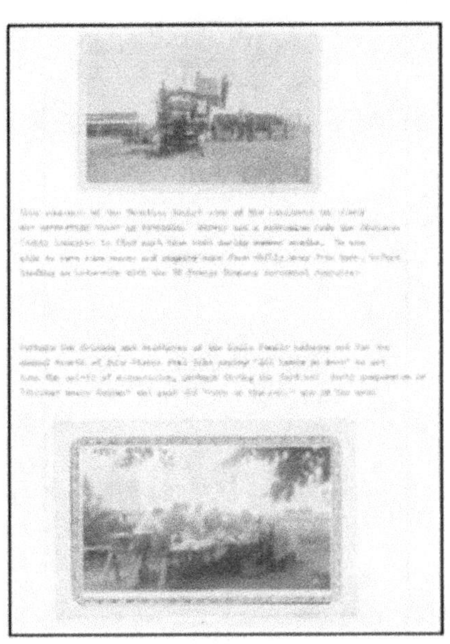

Perhaps the friends and relatives of the Didlo family helping out for the annual Fourth of July Picnic feel like saying "All hands on deck" to get into the spirit of cooperation, perhaps during the forties! Early preparation of "Chicken very Sunday" and good old "Corn on the cob." are on the menu.

This picture is Dad Didlo before he was a manager in later years… at an SS Kresge Store in Fort Madison, Iowa.

*Here is a photo of the editor before he was
able to tie his shoes very well.*

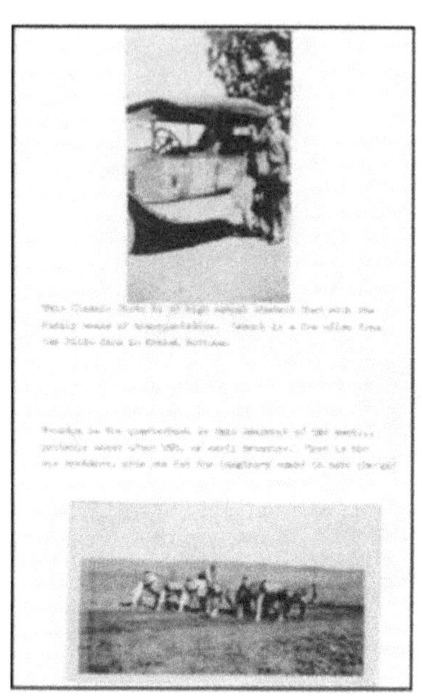

*This photo was taken about 1944 of
brother and sister...
Larry and Dee*

*Tobongganing on a Manitowoc, WI
hillside with
mom Claire in the early forties.*

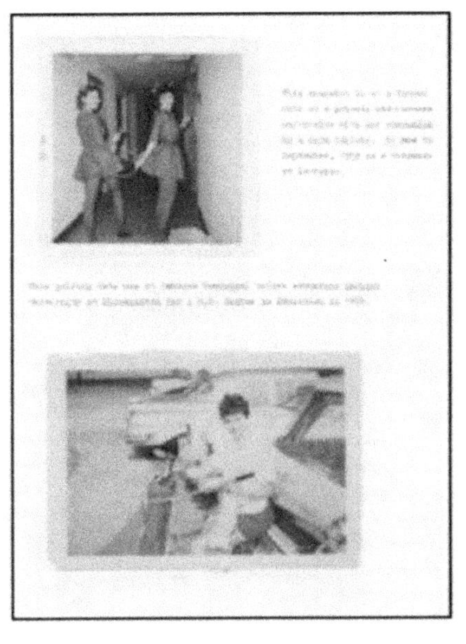

*First born of the "litter" in Manitowoc
is Dee pictured here with*

*mom and dad on a wooden double
swing. This photo was taken*

by a neighbor in 1939.

*This Classic Photo is of high school
student Chet with the family means of
transportation. School is a few miles
from the Didlo farm
in French Bottoms.*

About the Author

Although the author of this autobiography was my dad, I recently edited it to make it more interesting and readable. Therefore, for the sake of convenience, I Larry L. Didlo, am calling myself the author. There are three other E-books available through the Internet with IstBooks.com listed under my name. They are also associated with reading literacy and family life. This sixteen-page manuscript was written mostly over 21 years ago, six years before John Harvey Didlo passed away.

The editor-author grew up in Oshkosh with other family members after his dad was transferred from Manitowoc. Larry received the Eagle Badge when he was age 14 at the Manitowoc Kiwanis Club, and later the God & Country Award, after moving, at the Oshkosh Presbyterian Church with two other Eagle Scouts. While attending Oshkosh High School, he was elected President of the Student Council as a senior.

Later he received the B.S. Degree in secondary education with a major in Social Science from the school that is now called UW-O. He was a member of the National O Lettermans Club. In 1964 this educator, or editor-author (titles are sometimes confusing) was awarded a M.S. in Education at I.U. of Bloomington. His girlfriend helped him with the math portion of his major mid term paper. He taught full-time at the secondary level with the L.A. City School District for the first two years of his teaching career. Before going overseas, he was initiated in the PDK International Educational Fraternity in 1967. He is still active in Phi Delta Kappa today while secondary subbing at the Appleton Area School District. Before closing, I would like to mention my dad assisting adults to register to vote in Phoenix, as I did at Oshkosh Webster Stanley School 20 years later. Hats off to Mr. D. for a job well done!

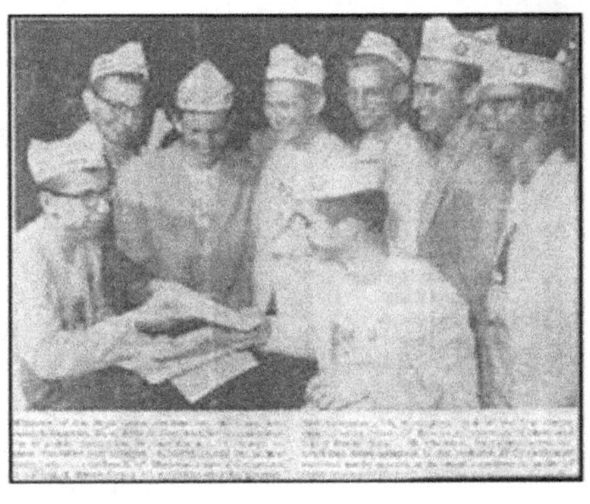

Boys', Girls' State
Delegates Named

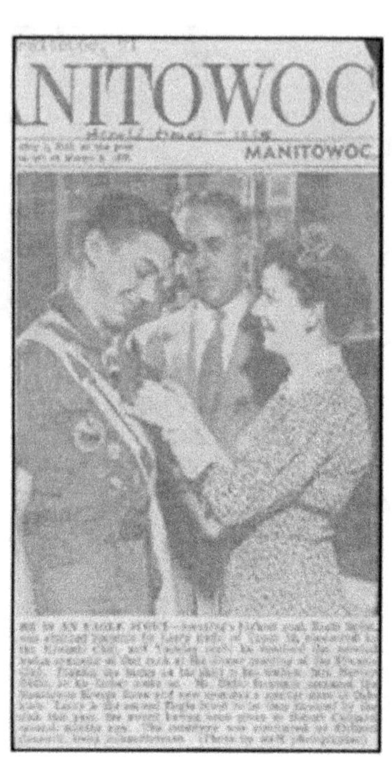

Services Recognize OHS '58 Graduates

DUEL FOR FIRST

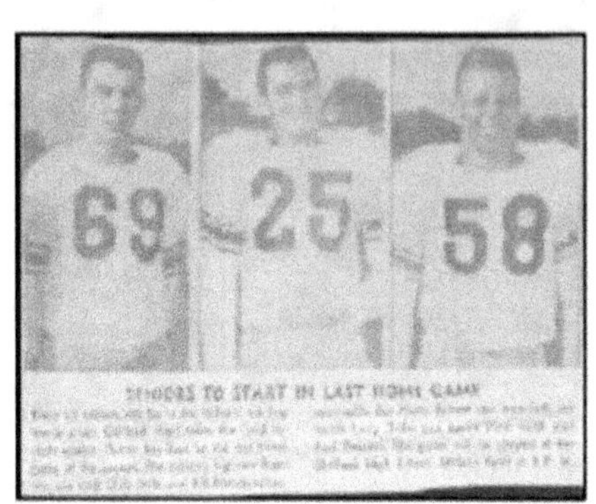

69 25 58
SENIORS TO START IN LAST HOME GAME

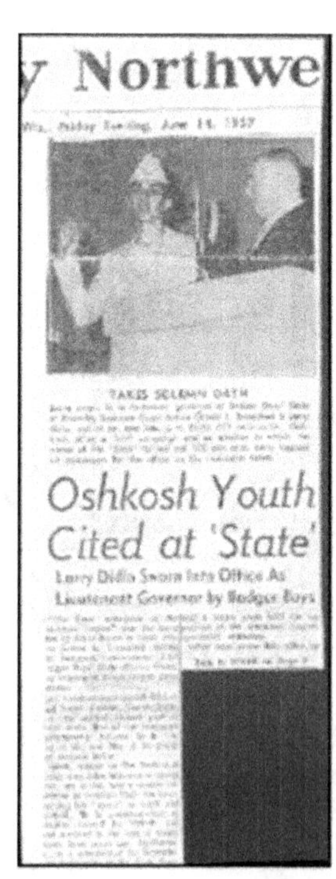

y Northwe
TAKES SOLEMN OATH
Oshkosh Youth
Cited at 'State'
Larry Diddis Sworn Into Office As
Lieutenant Governor by Badger Boys

Photo Essay & Reading Literacy

Larry L. Didlo

*The Didlo Family - growing up just after
WWII in Manitowoc, Wisconsin*

*Dad Didlo in his retirement years years after settling
in Oshkosh, Wisconsin.*

Scouting daze are clarified with a map indicating the northern route to Irvine Ranch, California - National Jamboree - from Manitowoc, Wisconsin.

Dad fishing-a-way at a neighbor's backyard.

Irvine Ranch, California-1953 National Boy Scout Jamboree-
Second Class Larry Didlo pounds a tent stake in the ground.

English Scouts visiting a London English Casle in December 1967.

Scouting daze are here again!

Mom takes a gander at Daisy Duck at Disneyland in Anaheim, California-1994-flying in from Phoenix, Arizona.

I was surprised at discovering a photo I took of my younger sister after moving from Manitowoc to Oshkosh my sophomore year in high school. The reading education department at UW-O gave me lots of ideas to pursue, when enrolled in the grad program.

"Settling down a spell" at a summer camp on the Chain of Lakes in Waupaca, Wisconsin with a friend.

Getting together before a high school dance in Oshkosh, Wisconsin with a date.

Boys state roommates explore Ripon College Campus while I was a delegate in 1957 from Oshkosh High School pursuing my photo hobby.

A High School track competition at the local Oshkosh athletic field kept me on my toes.

Badger Boys marching on campus is a common experience throughout the nation for a week each year.

Junior High School Team Manitowoc, Wisconsin.

*Seattle World's Fair in 1962. Christian Evangelical
Pavilion to the right.*

*Touring the "Palais De Versailles" in Paris on my school
Thanksgiving vacation when teaching overseas in 1967-68.*

*A new arrival at St. Paul's Cathedral in London, England late
in December 1967 on my Christmas vacation from teaching
overseas at an Army dependants School in Europe.*

Delivering a graduation speech at high school commencement in Oshkosh lat in the fifties.

Earning my way through college during the summer after high school graduation.

*My first experience was at Venice Elementary
as a teacher, starting out in Los Angeles.*

*I transferred to a J.H.S. near Santa Monica, California
after a week or two at Venice Elementary.*

Active duty in Pacific Northwest in early 60's.

Souvenir from Walworth County area while on faculty of high school in late 60's.

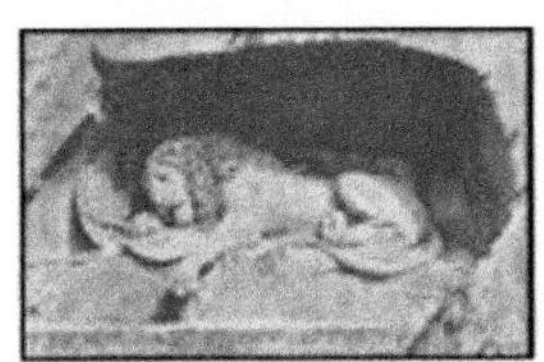

*Here's a souvenir postcard from Switzerland purchased
while serving as a JHS camp counselor at Davos, Switzerland
in summer, 1968.*

*A visitor poses at the Paine Art Center in Oshkosh
to take a closer look at a senior's project for the
25th Anniversary of O.S.C. 2000 AD.*

*As a graduate student (at I.U., Bloomington, Indiana)
I snapped this photo of a popular campus tourist spot in 1967.*

A Daily ritual at church camp (Onaway Island) at Waupaca, Wisconsin.

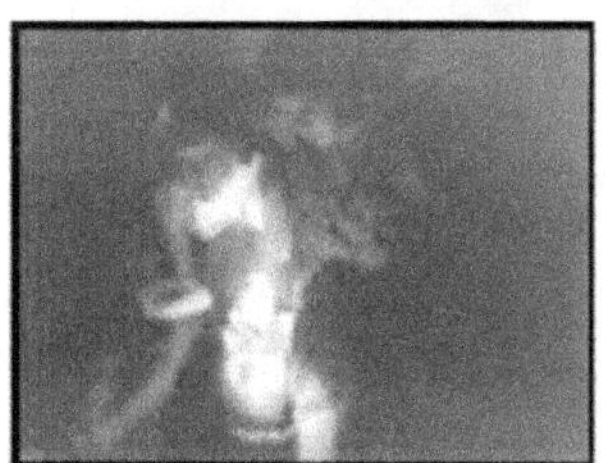

Halloween 1960-younger sister and neighbor girl.

New additions to our family tree - Christmas 1999.

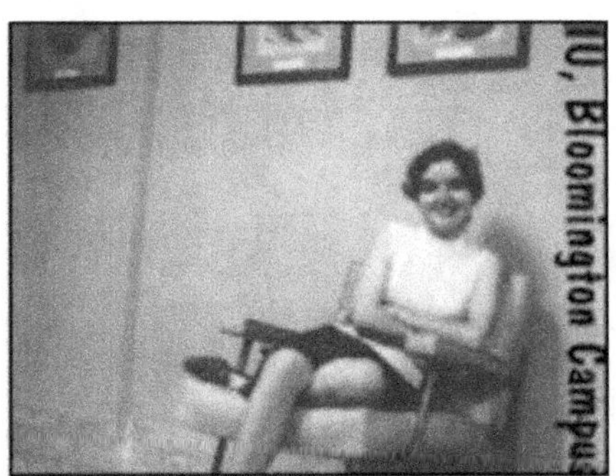

*Fellow grad student in education field visited I.U campus
in 1964.*

Caravan sponsored by the First Presbyterian Church of Oshkosh, WI summer of 1967.

Stopped overnight in Minneapolis, Minnesota at affiliate church-about 12 crew members.

Sisseton, South Dakota

Living pictures related to reading literary perspective.

Here is one of the favorite side shows at Oshkoah's Sawdust Days this Millennium year, July 4, 2000. Feeding time for Tony!

Class speakerts of OHS '68

*The "Mark Twain" was a favorite ride at
Anaheim (Disneyland) in our visit (mid 90's)
to California.*

*Apples on the back porch of younger brother Bill's Apple
orchard-we made a few gallons of apple juice one Sunday afternoon
(late 90's) and gave them to neighbors.*

Woodcraft Hobby mid 90's.

Messenger of Transformation

A storm is off the coastal shore. In the midst of dark clouds and sun, flies a seagull bound for shore.

A messenger of hope for those who are cast at sea — A symbol of peace and light during the midst of storm, a bird of fight.

It flies forward and points the way for the daybreak of a new dawn.

The Great Bird Above

Oh majestic birds of wonder — Glide with me and soar beyond the mountain peaks.

Lift my spirits with your sight and bring me back to the earth's crust safely.

Abide with care and kindness knowing that you're special to me.

Ode to Captain of the Helm

Over hill, over dale, while my Red Rover purrs about. With the Lord in my heart and hand on the wheel, the sunshine lights the forward path.

Lead on oh knighted driver and look on thy neighbor as one special enroute — with a bluebird on your shoulder.

A Mouse on the Scene

Mickey, the Camelot Cat, visits the Holiday Jamestown Caper with Captain John Smith. Halloween has just passed. Mickey, somewhat the Noble Knight from Nottingham, came in by American ship to visit John Smith near '76. He was guided by a flock of honking geese near Canada at night, and day by shore with a seafaring seagull. It looks as if a pilgrim's Thanksgiving was soon to pass, table all prepared, with or without the Indian Maiden Pocahontas. Winter frost was near— pumpkins ready for harvest.

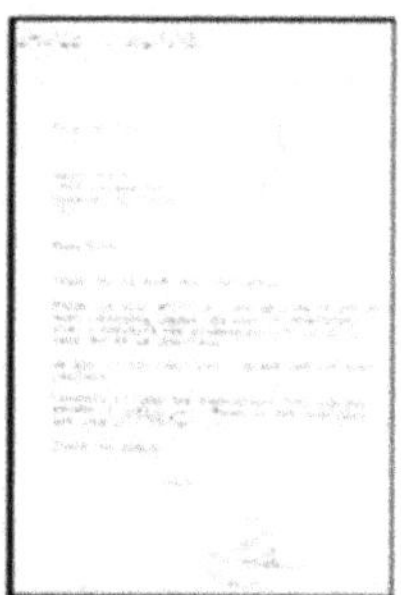

DEATH

The black crowa began circling from above— Their cawing pierced the evening air with fear.

The scavengers were eyeing their prey below— A rabbit smashed on the highway by the rushing truck.

COFFEE

The coffee grounds, like sand in the desert

Made a swirling pattern in the bottom of the trashcan.

Day is done, another reawakening tomorrow—

The smell and aroma wait for us, while we anticipate

Another flavor for tomorrow!

PITER - PATTER

The water was coming down in small droplets, threshing

The puddles in reoccuring concentric circles, ever widening.

The morning was bright with the rising sun, while the clouds

Were layered upon one another.

Another day greets us with a robinson's chirping, fresh and pure.

ALERT

Lightening bolts struck and staggered throughout the evening dusk...

Hurricane weather was alerting us to be cautious!

The wind outside was swirling and gusting every which way.

Downstairs the family huddles together, with a transistor radio on—

A hush on making noise is in effect.

When can we go upstairs and turn the lights back on;

Our candles flame is flickering? When will we resume the night's calm?

TIC TOC

The clocks pendulum swings; methodically marking out the progress of the grandfather clock menagerie...

A silhouette of circus animal figures, no mouse stirring or fast asleep.

In the kitchen there seems to be a background of sound of drips from the faucet. The dishes are all done.

A slight breeze is filtered through the bedroom's screen making a whizzing sound.

Yes Grandfather is home! He is keeping time with the evening symphony of sounds...

Seated in his creaking pine rocking chair.

Poems resemble Haiku content and briefness, bringing out sounds, nature, and inner calmness. Thid graduate student attempts to put himself in the shoes of the learner-a co-learner with his student he is tutoring. The writer of poems doesn't expect to get rich writing poetry, but tries to create an inner picture of reality using imagery of simplicity and senses.

I found that working and teaching overseas, that educators, businessmen, parents alike, must simply discard or cast aside their religious designations, and act as peacemakers, and ambassadors of goodwill in and out of their classrooms.

After accepting the 1967-68 overseas international faculty position (under the Johnson Administration), I discovered that a warm bowl of oatmeal for breakfast could make difference between success or failure — especially in reading alertness and comprehension!

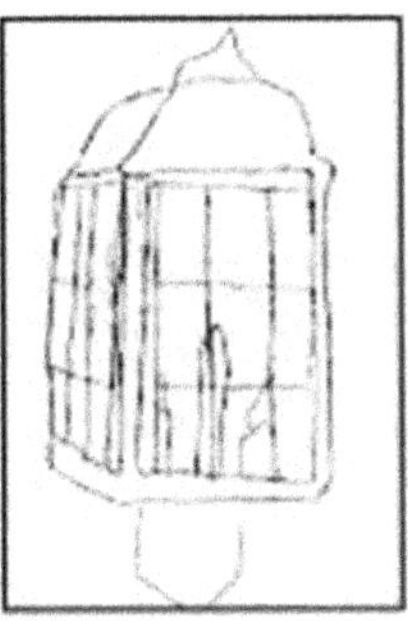

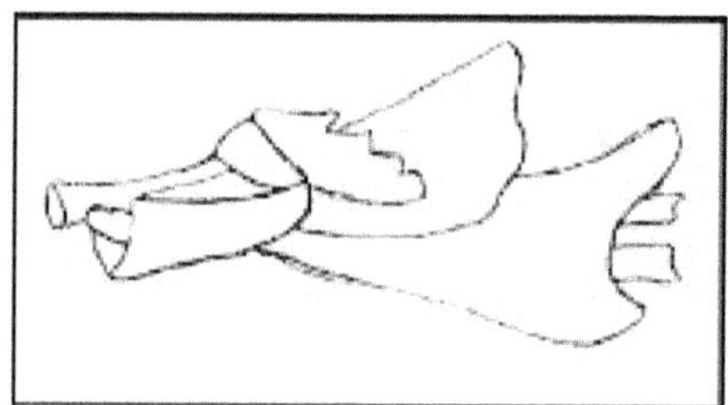

*Christmas theme designs for scroll saw patterns
or perhaps wood burning projects.*

Commit Thy Way
Unto the Lord

BADGER
BOYS STATE

FORMAL INAUGURAL
CEREMONY
JUNE 13, 1957 8:15 P.M.
RIPON COLLEGE

THE PENALTY OF *Leadership*

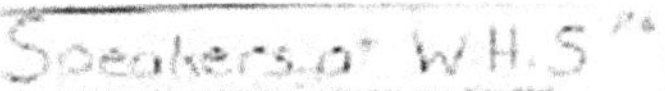

JUNIOR-SENIOR
PROM

Community Activities and Reading Boost Career Development

By: Larry Didlo, Oshkosh WI

Writing this article gives me a chance to reflect on past early travel and related educational experience. I'm writing from the advantage point of being a former guidance counselor and social studies teacher in a secondary school setting. I also studied reading education at the University of Wisconsin-Oshkosh during night school. I'm certified in reading education and am currently a WSRA and Fox Valley Reading Council member. The main purpose or focus of this article is to discuss how community involvement helps students with reading and careers, as it has me.

First, the Boy Scouts, on the Eagle Trail, or pathways, began early for me with Cub Scout involvement and interest. A National Jamboree sparked enthusiasm for the world wide scouting movement. It promoted interest in travel and education. On the way to California, several years ago, to a National Scouting Jamboree, our group stopped at Yellowstone for sight-seeing.

Swapping tents, and outdoor camping and cooking, including mass hillside gatherings were part of the Irvine Ranch experience close to the ocean shore. The then Vice-president, Nixon, spoke before several thousand scouts about the importance of teamwork and scouting, followed by a skit about the three musketeers. President Eisenhower was scheduled to speak but had a time conflict. Interest in social studies for me continued from this point, and more scouting experiences gave more depth of understanding in preparing lessons and coaching, especially in the role as a teacher-counselor with overseas dependents Department of Defense Schools in Europe. For example, I learned from Scouting that modeling or demonstrating is an important ingredient for success, not only in reading, but in sports as well.

Earning merit badges while in junior high and later educational endeavors contributed to the following: (1) teaching secondary social studies, (2) instructing swimming skills with the American Red Cross, and (3) participating in such civic organizations as the American Legion. Presently, I am a substitute teacher concentrating on reading and social studies.

I have found reading is associated with the out-of-doors just as it is related to such indoor experiences as home video games. Therefore our milieu is a variable, and ususally printed material is associated with getting started in comprehension and serves as a valuable reference.

Working toward the Boy Scouts of America Lifesaving Badge at the Wisconsin YMCA Camp Anokijig was another valuable experience. There at Plymouth, with another scout, I learned the importance of the scouting motto anf further education.

Retirement from teaching in the East Central Wisconsin region looms before me in the next ten years. However, membership in the National Eagle Scout Association (NESA) contributes to my being an informal representative of the local scouting program for the older boys. Interest in reading and scouting activities enhance part time teaching, in addition to helping me to be a better merit badge counselor. In conclusion, it seems that travel and positive social experiences whether in scouting or whatever, all assist one to set and help reach reasonable self fulfilling goals as a teacher or student.

> "The main purpose or focus of this article is to discuss how community involvement helps students with reading and careers, as it has me."

Partnership of Literacy

1996 Convention

Wisconsin State Reading Association

40th Anniversary

This article is a reprint (retyped) published in Winter 1995-96 by Wisconsin State Reading Association.

It was published in a Secondary Reading Newsletter named Focus, Vol. II, No. 1 Biannual and by the same author.

CROSSROADS OF LITERACY: TECHNOLOGY AND EDUCATION

Copyright 2000, Larry L. Didlo

This book may not be reproduced in any form without written consent of the author.

LET'S PRETEND:
KINDERGARTEN-JET FLIGHT

How can kindergarten teachers get their children more involved in the reading experience and process? How can they make the reading process more enjoyable, and be a plus for <u>literacy</u> in their approach?

The last few years I've been a docent (volunteer exhibit guide of sorts) at the local Experimental Aircraft Association Museum in Oshkosh. For favorites, I chose the Voyager and Johnson Wax Sikorsky Replica Exhibits. The amphibian plane of the 30's holds about a dozen passengers for a simulated flight of ten minutes. They travel to the wax palms of Brazil and are met by natives. Perhaps a kindergarten jet role-playing experience would serve as an introduction to such a museum visit. A literacy-oriented play could he planned composed of 5 1/2 year olds pretending to fly to Disneyland. Literacy could be embedded in some event or planned experience for the child! This might lie the necessary closure or cognitive challenge that they could all relate to and serve as the thread, glue, whatever to unite life long goals. This approach might be more balanced with a reading project involving phonics, listening, writing, speaking, literature, and centered around some noteworthy event. The students would be motivated to learn more about reading because it involves play; the play factor being key to the whole role-playing reading situation.

First, the teacher at the local community Y, Boys and Girls Club, public or private school could help a student role play using the phone to call their travel agent. She could make the necessary choices for arrangements to buy tickets for a certain date in front of classmates. For example, if the group were transferring planes in Denver, the supervisor might talk about the possibility of a baggage handlers strike. After arranging for tickets on a particular date to Disneyland, the class might role-play the experience of flying. There might be music involved with pretend tea drinking. The plane boarded might be made of a double column of chairs, two boards for the wings centered on end tables or file cabinets, with two or four table fans to stimulate the props or jets on the outspread wings made of two boards. The pilot would be in front with his navigator in the cockpit wearing a cap perhaps, and identified by calling him

Captain (Lindberg) of Mr. Wright (Orville or Wilber).

Since California is the home of Disney land and a long ways from Wisconsin, permission must be received from the passenger (Kindergarten students) parents. An open letter could he drafted by the teacher with student response and suggestions on the class easel with a marker. The students would supposedly have to take the letter home and get their parents signature for the simulated journey. They might then watch the inspector' student chosen, of the homemade jet replica, check the plane for possible mending (Mr. Pipe would be his name with a sign so indicating hung around his neck).

Perhaps there could be a group discussion on what to pack and remind them to take a bar of soap! Also, they might want to vote on whether they want to begin their theme-park visit by going first to the Abe Lincoln exhibit. Variations to the above suggestions would be dependent on the class's level and experience in travel, and the teacher's inguity! After the pretend trip was over, a class note to the local newspaper, on the easel again, could be written discussing favorite rides such as the Mark Twain Paddle wheeler. The city would be thanked publicly for allowing the airport to operate with a letter to 'The Editors Column.' The focus of this article has been a more practical approach, or literate approach toward reading at a sensitive age of learning.

READING READINESS AND VIDEO GAMES

Everyday parents are becoming more important in the preschool educational process. Although video games do not take the place of reading individually to one's child, they can be good motivators and assist in the reading process if used with dicretion. The younger student's interact with the colorful graphics, and sound effects of the TV monitor with fingers and sight. Early keyboarding skills enhance later artwork, writing skills, and numbering used in math. Computer keyboarding can be improved by having used the video game controls at home of school.

As a reading supervisor employed substitute presently, it is my opinion that early exposure to this electronic phenomena puts fun, if nothing else, back into the learning process. Parents should supervise and preview the games just like the classroom teacher, coach, what have you, does with computer software and A-V Aids. It's parent's responsibility to make available a variety of reading experiences involved in reading readiness at an early age.

Some guidelines without using commercial name are as follows: (I) Consider appropriate age level and interest when renting, or purchasing the interactive games, (2) Choose a variety of subjects, (3) Model and preview games just as one does with books for children before presenting individually to students, (4) Be aware of appropriate time limits, encouraging 15 minute breaks, nutrition etc. As an adult reader talk to the young player about his progress and levels reached in the game.

Whether or not interactive video games will become a part of the away-from home education experience at school, will remain to be seen. However, parental and teacher roles can be enriching and self-fulfilling in themselves.

I have found that electronic video games fit in well with my two 'guinea pigs' so to speak... relatives, a boy and girl under 7. Their schedule and attention span are involved, and they do quite well. Proper involvement seems to promote concentration and interest in pre and post reading skill development.

Perhaps video interactive games will he made available at school as the computer Internet is someday for achievers as well as the less gifted. Philosophically the interaction aspects of such electronic systems ties in with the learning is experience theme. As an educator, I believe we are only at the tip of the iceberg, when it comes to using advanced technology at home and in the school classroom.

RUNNING WITH JESUS

As a high school athlete competing in track events, I discovered that being Moderator of the local Westminster Sn. High Fellowship strengtened my Faith... increasing trust in others and myself. Having faith and confidence in self as an athlete, or hurdle for example, gave me extra strength and agility to almost break the 120-yard high hurdle local school record of 14.5 seconds. During that partiular meet and day I came within 1/10th of a second away from the local high school record. There was a slight breeze behind me that afternoon. I recall that my H.S Guidance Counselor shot the starting gun, and the school principal assisted in holding the finishing tape, congratulating me for the nice win that very special day.

Such Olympians as Johnny Weissmuller, Jim Thorpe, and Jesse Owens were all sports mentors for me about 35 years ago.

Although this particular race of my high school track career enabled me to compete at the Wisconsin State Track Meet in Milwaukee, unfortunately during the first qualifying heat, I fell while going over the second hurdle of the highs. Luckily I got up unijured... only dazed and somewhat shaken!

Later in college at Oshkosh, while representing the Titans at the Beloit Invitational Meet of '61, I won a well-crafted silver medal. Our four-man hurdle team won second place away from home.

Starting in Manito Wilson JHS while working out and training over eight or nine years (later moving to Oshkosh), I felt that such practice was a worthy effort with individual rewards as well. Rewards as better health, staying in shape, meeting fellow students in atheletic competition from other cities, higher self esteem, and eventual membership in the National Titan 'O' Club (UW—O Varsity Letter Winners) justifies the sustained effort.

Therefore, in conclusions, I would hope to finish on a positive note. If one does not shut God out in one's life, he is more apt to live up to his potential. Perhaps this is true whether competing in inter-scholastic sports, on-the-job experiences, or just living out life's great challenges. This sort of explains why this theme or article could be associated with just plain POSITIVE THINK-ING.

God makes sense in school and life. Competing in sports is just one arena where catching the spirit or enthusiasm seems more apparent. Volunteering for worthy community projects is another area of humanitarian endeavor.

Competing in sports at school, Badger Boys State, Army Basic Training competitive sports at Fort Leonard Wood for me, and such events as University sponsored Greek Society Track Meets, provided me with a more structured developmental learning situation based on competition and good sportsmanship.

As a secondary educator and track coach, partime YMCA Life Saving Instructor, and voluntary Red Cross First Aid Instructor, I found my early sports competitive experiences assisted in molding me into a more effective communicator, or facilitator, and coach. As the Bible states, "One can do all things in which Christ strengthens him." Such a statement probably should be underlined because it gives us hope and direction for our motivation and often undiscovered potential.

This article was written to be considered as an eventual published article in a religious or inspirational format. It was written in Phoenix, Arizona while vacationing-near Easter 1997 as a real life experience which served as a building block for future development in the field of education. St. Lawrence Consortium Educational Foundation chief editor, Larry Didlo and writer of article, STE 8443, 1880 Jackson Street, Oshkosh, WI, 54901.

A CAREER PERSPECTIVE: ONE STEP AT A TIME

A student, or scouter, should begin thinking about college and careers probably as early as JHS. This enable one to take the proper course sequence in school and sort of gives direction to one's extra-curricular activities. Such words as patience, and persistence seem to ring a hell, or at least help along the way, as does diversifying time and talents. Getting as much post high school education as possible seems to be a good start. It will be more apt to lead one to self-fulfillment and accomplishment, and higher quality of life. I would recommend volunteering for the Peace Corps, or military service, after a year or two of college, or degree, if it relates to your career plans, or interest. Such experience would also give one a more balanced perspective toward the world of work in which we live. Work experience during college promotes self-insight, education on a more practical level, and pays for students expenses.

What about marriage? Marriage will take care of itself, if one starts the wheels turning by enrolling in college. BEING PREPARED seems applicable as a motto in scouting years as well in college. Camp counseling, for example, might be helpful in preparing for an educational career with young people, whether it be with the YMCA, Scouts, or church camp setting. I recall my overseas camp counseling experience in Switzerland in an international setting very interesting and challenging.

More students are enrolling in college, or universities, than ever before. It is important to set your priorities first before high school. Scouting experience helps. If you find success in sports for example, this might be an indication you'd be successful as a coach in an educational setting.

As an active member of NESA (National Eagle Scout Associaton) for several years, I believe there are reciprocal relationships between scouting, higher education, and success. Although one doesn't necessarily gauge success by the dollar sign, a more stable and higher quality of life is insured if one shoots for the stars so to speak, not being content with just being average. Also, along the way toward a more meaningful life and experience, you may wish to sharpen your public speaking skills with a dale Carnegie Public Speaking Course locally, and/or listen to Nightengale-Contant LEAD THE FIELD Tapes. As a secondary substitute public school teacher, I seem to come to the conclusion that the American People are becoming more visually oriented, with TV News Broadcasters and all. However, more in-depth reading comes with being motivated or interested in a subject as conversation... somewhat self-generated. Soaring the heights by pursuing the Eagle Scout Badge seems to be a wise decision in preparing for the future.

UNLOCKING ENLIGHTENED SPLENDOR

About thirty years ago I learned an important lesson in life, which helped me unlock my hidden potential, in serving the Lord. While pursuing a higher degree in the field of education at a Big Ten University in the Midwest, I became aware of how Jesus Christ was using me in one of many ways for service to His Church. There away from home, I joined the local church's choir of my denomination, after being initiated in PDK, which was a professional educational fraternity for me and women on campus.

Although I never received my M.S. in Education Degree, with the traditional pomp and circumstance or ceremony, due to other commitments that summer, singing in the choir at a small midwestern church's choir near campus, gave me the opportunity to see God's wisdom at work, even though we don't always completely understand Him when younger. Unfortunately being in my mid-fifties presently, I still haven't found Miss or the future Mrs. Right. I don't think I'll be another St. Paul, but marriage still may be in the cards, or possibility for me. Where would Billy Graham or Bill Clinton be without their wives today?

Reading "PLUS, The Magazine of Positive Thinking," and skimming through my mother's book entitled, <u>My Utmost for His Highest</u> helps me also unlock ENLIGHTENED SPLENDOR from the wisdom of other's pens and emotions. Sometimes I look back upon my life and think how much I've missed with no wife or children. However, then I reflect on Baden Powell's successful marriage with children, late in life and how much he influenced young people by starting the ball rolling, or founding the scout movement around the globe. It's never too late to begin. As an active scouting volunteer, American Legion member, plus subbing in secondary schools, I realize that graduating from a merit badge counselor to perhaps assistant scoutmaster, or resource consultant, mauy be just over the horizon or hill to accomplish. For example, seeing the growth and progress of my great nephew at his Cub Scout's softball workout and practice, at the local public school, is just one of my outgrowths of service with a smile. Certainly we are constantly in the midst of being challenged by our Lord, in unlocking our hidden potential in discovering God's Grace in service towards others, while we have the opportunity to live in such an exciting and ever changing society.

Larry L. Didlo

STE 8443 - 1880 Jackson Street

Oshkosh, WI 54901

Submitted to Norman Vincent Peale's PLUS Magazine for possible publication on May 21st, 1997